JUDO ARMBARS
FOR MIXED MARTIAL ARTS

JUDO ARMBARS
FOR MIXED MARTIAL ARTS

DOMINIC KING
4th Dan Black Belt and Professional MMA Coach

RETHINK PRESS

First published in Great Britain 2015
by Rethink Press (www.rethinkpress.com)

"...it felt as though my arm was being ripped away from my body!"

Dominic King describes what it was like to be on the receiving end of the great Neil Adams' favourite technique—the juji gatame roll.

ACKNOWLEDGEMENTS

My first thank you needs to go to Joe Gregory, a former student of mine in both judo and MMA. Joe quickly became a friend and I am now also proud to call him my publisher. When Joe suggested one day that I should write a book on what I do best, I initially laughed, although secretly I had always fancied writing a book, but never seriously expected it to happen.

Secondly I would like to thank Shaun Brooks for providing some great action shots for the book. Shaun is a high level sports photographer who spends a great deal of his time at Wembley and other major football grounds and sports arenas, taking photographs of some of the country's best known faces.

Also thanks to Steven Webster of East Coast Black Belt School for allowing us to use their fantastic facility.

Unrelated to the book, I think it is important to thank my former training partners and coaches for their contribution to my career, in particular my first judo coach, Mel Church and my most recent coach, Nigel Thompson, who helped me a great deal to progress to a high level.

As in all high level sport it is inevitable that at some point injuries will occur and throughout my career I received my fair share of injuries. If it wasn't for my physio Steve Foster, it is likely that I would have missed some vital competitions along the way, so I would like to say a big thank you to the Foster Clinic for their continuous support and sponsorship over the previous 20 years.

I would like to thank my understanding older brother, Adam, for his constant support despite having judo rammed down his throat 24/7 and for never complaining when I took all the praise.

To my mum I want to say thanks for the thousands of packed lunches she must have made over the years and for being a sympathetic ear when things were not going in my favour.

I want to thank my wife and best friend, Claire, for the fantastic 18 years spent together and for the support and sacrifice as she constantly put her life on hold while I pursued my dream.

However, the biggest thank you should go to my dad for being my judo coach, my driver, my photographer, my video man, my secretary, my bank manager/ financial advisor, my news reporter, my water boy, my psychologist, my life coach, my head of IT, my number one fan, my critic and my friend. He has been there from start to finish and truly has the commitment of a champion.

FOREWORD
by Emma 'Heavy D' Delaney

Anyone hoping to be in with a chance of beating Dom in a judo competition would need to be technically, physically and mentally strong, as well as fit enough to last the duration. At the beginning of the day, you could guarantee that Dom would be standing on the rostrum in arguably the strongest men's weight category, the under 66kgs.

I have known Dom for more than 15 years and followed his career mainly from the opposite coach's chair during national events, but also as a fellow British squad member and as a friend. I have total respect for Dom as a fighter and would often refer to him as one of 'the most technical' fighters in the UK. Now in retirement, Dom is putting his vast knowledge to good use by coaching the next generation, but like myself and a few others, Dom has decided to take a slightly different path into the world of mixed martial arts (MMA). Dom has worked hard to understand how his judo skills can be used in the cage and with his natural ability and dedication to drill new techniques, he has added to his game and made a successful transition to MMA.

As a former International judoka and now a professional MMA fighter with 'Cage Warriors', I also understand the importance of technical drills. I often find myself screaming at cage side or at the TV when I can see an obvious opportunity for a judo technique that I have drilled countless times, although many judo attacks are not commonly used in the cage and this is why I believe they are often effective.

A technique that is often seen on the judo mat is the 'juji gatame' which MMA fans refer to simply as the 'armbar'. This technique has been made notorious in recent years by the UFC Undisputed Bantamweight Champion, Ronda Rousey, who won a string of professional MMA bouts using the move. In 22 years of judo I can claim that I have never tapped from an armbar which is largely due to drilling a defensive move to the technique.

This book will serve as a useful tool for any fighter regardless of their background or level of ability, as Dom unlocks some of the most sought after answers in MMA today.

CONTENTS

CHAPTER ONE
Introduction

If you're looking for a way to enhance your fight game, then incorporating judo armbars into your MMA arsenal is a really good way to go. The straight armbar, or juji gatame, is one of the most effective and fastest submissions in the cage.

However, a lot of MMA fighters dismiss traditional martial arts such as judo because of the associated formalities and rituals. These guys are missing out on being able to develop and master this devastating technique because they haven't looked beyond the gi, the belts and the bowing.

The techniques, the training methods and skills you can acquire from judo can give you a significant edge over a purely MMA focused fighter, however, you're not normally going to get exposure to these elements without having to go through years of formal training.

This is the challenge and this is where I can help.

When a traditional martial artist like myself understands the game of MMA and has taken the steps to acquire skills and knowledge to become an all round fighter, they can see where aspects of their traditional martial art can be effectively applied in MMA and can pass those insights on when coaching.

That's what I've done with this book.

I had my first judo lesson when I was four years old—that was nearly 35 years ago. As a judo fighter I competed at a high level, winning the British Championship in 2001 and the Youth Olympic silver medal in 1995. I've also beaten several Olympians throughout my career and I recall watching the medal ceremony at the 2002 Commonwealth Games, only to realise that I had beaten everyone on the rostrum.

I trained hard, was always extremely motivated and was able to bounce back from injuries and overcome setbacks. I also felt a strong desire to win and during my time as a full time athlete I thought of little else. After my career as an Olympic contender came to a premature end due to ill health, I became a professional judo coach in 2004.

Seeing the increasing demand from MMA fighters for world-class grappling skills, I opened an MMA club in 2010 with the help of established striking coaches. However, my judo career has allowed my path to cross with a number of today's top MMA fighters including UFC fighters and some pioneers of the sport in this country as far back as the nineties. So I have always been aware of the sport and followed the careers of my friends, as well as learning a number of techniques that are not traditionally used in judo.

So, despite never becoming a UFC fighter, or even an Olympian for that matter, I would feel comfortable teaching my grappling skills to UFC standard fighters because the techniques that I have adapted for MMA allow them to benefit from aspects of traditional judo without having to spend 35 years training in the art.

CHAPTER TWO
Judo in the Cage

After judo was introduced into the Olympic Games in 1964, its popularity steadily increased worldwide. However, during the 1970s, 80s and 90s, judo experienced some problems. Those problems were known as Bruce Lee, Jackie Chan, Jean Claude Van-Damme, The Karate Kid, The Ninja Turtles and The Power Rangers. All were great martial artists and they all looked fantastic on screen, but there wasn't a single grappler within this group of famous fighters. The audience loved them, but it seemed that people often overlooked the fact that they were fictional characters and believed everything they saw on screen. Some may argue that Bruce, Jackie and Jean Claude were actually expert martial artists in real life, a statement I couldn't disagree with, but I could guarantee that in a real life situation, their fighting styles would be very different from their on screen characters. You have to ask yourself why a flying spinning kick almost never happens in MMA and why a back flip is non existent. However, prior to the MMA era, everyone was sucked in by the movies, with boxing, karate and kung fu definitely winning the popularity contest.

Throughout the eighties and nineties I steadily developed some recognition locally by appearing in newspapers and even on area news programs, as more and more results came my way. However, I lost count of the times I was approached by people who wanted me to demonstrate a kick or a chop and on occasions I would get jokers square up to me accompanied by the Bruce Lee sound effects, which I am sure every judo fighter has experienced at one time or another. Sometimes I would correct them but mostly I just let them get on with it. Finding out that judo involved no form of striking would normally be accompanied with a face that suggested that judo must be easy, like a Mickey Mouse version of karate. Even the fact that judo was an Olympic sport often did it no favours, as in those days, with all minority sports getting a tiny amount of television coverage, you would see a few minutes of a final match. However the best two fighters in the world would not always make for the most exciting contest, especially to the untrained spectator, as their abilities were so great that they would often cancel each other out. Terry Wogan once said that judo was like watching two grown men cuddling in pyjamas!

Japanese judo fighters may well have been household names, but in the UK that was certainly not the case. Neil Adams was our equivalent to Steve Redgrave who was World Champion in the 80s and one of the best technicians of all time, but unlike Redgrave, he unexpectedly lost two Olympic finals back to back so never received the recognition he deserved.

A British judo fighter from the seventies made more of an impact during the eighties, but not for judo. Brian Jacks built his reputation from his unbeatable performances on the popular television show 'Superstars', which saw the country's best athletes go head to head in a multi event contest to find the best sportsman in the land. Jacks demolished the opposition, including double Olympic Champion decathlete Daley Thompson. Jacks was considered a machine and produced over 100 dips in one minute while his opponents were struggling to achieve half as many. Jacks had his 15 minutes of fame, although I'm still sure that a lot of the viewers assumed that he was a karate fighter anyway.

This up hill struggle for the grapplers would continue until the Ultimate Fighting Championship emerged in 1993. The early days of the UFC were fought in a tournament format with the winners of each contestant progressing though the rounds until one warrior stood alone as the victor. The tournament included fighters with a wide variety of styles as one art clashed against another. The event was truly fascinating as, for the first time, arguments about which art would be more effective than another were settled. It came as a shock to a large number of people that the victor was not a Mike Tyson or even a Bruce Lee type, but a Brazilian guy wearing pyjamas! The Champion was Royce Gracie—a Brazilian Jiu Jitsu fighter from a large soon to be famous family of fighters from which Royce was one of several and not considered the best of the bunch. Royce's strategy for the tournament was simply this: Low kick the knee to maintain the distance, shoot for the opponent's legs when the time was right

and demolish them on the ground with chokes or armbars. Simple strategy, but it worked in every contest without him even breaking a sweat. Most people changed their opinion about grappling from then on, but even to this day there are still some naïve fighters and spectators who believe that a world class boxer would simply finish a no holds barred contest with one punch every time. One of those people was World Champion boxer James Toney, who was confident enough to put that theory to the test by taking on UFC legend Randy Couture. Randy, an ex Greco Roman wrestler took seconds to take Toney to the floor with a basic wrestling move and submitted the boxer with the simplest of chokes.

Nowadays, very few fighters enter the cage without some form of grappling knowledge, although to be fair, it is just as unwise to compete without any striking ability. The sport of MMA has evolved so much since 1993 and all fighters are well prepared with a variety of takedown defences as well as techniques to stand back up if a takedown is successful.

Most MMA fighters today practise Brazilian Jiu Jitsu on a regular basis. As it has been successfully tried and tested over many years, this is a wise decision. However, judo, which is also very effective in the cage has often been overlooked, as freestyle wrestling is often used to take opponents to the floor. This is hardly surprising with the popularity of MMA in America, where a large number of children and young adults participate in freestyle wrestling at school and college. Most top judo fighters usually prefer to stick to the traditional game, with their ultimate target being the Olympic gold medal. BJJ has evolved with MMA in mind and wrestling is being adapted for MMA more and more, especially since its exclusion from future Olympic Games. Judo on the other hand has taken longer to adapt although a rising number of judoka are making the transition to MMA as its popularity increases.

The 1992 Olympic Champion, Hidehiko Yoshida, was the first big name judoka to try his luck in MMA. His match up against the original UFC Champion, Royce Gracie, was the first match up of its kind since the great judoka Masahiko Kimura took on Brazilian Jiu Jitsu founder Helio Gracie in 1951. Kimura won that particular battle with a submission that was later named after him and is a move that is commonly used by MMA and BJJ fighters today. Like Kimura before him, Yoshida won the match up, but this time by a strangle. (A strangle that I use very successfully against Jiu Jitsu fighters). Royce claimed that he didn't tap, which is correct – correct only because he was unconscious and was unable to do so! To be fair to Gracie, he did win their rematch by a decision, which was probably helped by the fact that he wisely removed his gi jacket before the bout, making it more difficult for Yoshida to attempt his world class throws. Yoshida went on to fight some of the top MMA fighters in the world and finished with a decent enough record.

While Yoshida made his mark within the Japanese 'Pride' organisation, its American rival, the 'UFC' had found its own judo star, in the shape of Karo Parisyan. Karo was not a big judo name like Yoshida, but he was very good, with a strong record in the American National Championships and had been unlucky not to compete in the Olympic Games. However, unlike any other judo fighter before him, Parisyan was able to adapt his judo skills beautifully for the non gi wrestling aspect of MMA. From an early age he had entered no gi grappling tournaments and had taken to the cage against adults at just 14 years old. He spent his early years in a tough area of Armenia before moving to Los Angeles with his parents, where things didn't get any easier for the young Karo. Caught in an ongoing feud between Armenians and Mexicans, Parisyan would fight on a regular basis and things became so bad that eight of his friends lost their lives in gang related incidents. The mentality that develops as a result of this type of upbringing is impossible to learn in a gym or a dojo and many great fighters through the years have come from similar backgrounds —Mike Tyson to name just one.

Before MMA burst onto the scene, Tyson was considered by most people as the ultimate fighting machine and there were very few arguments to claim otherwise. With the benefit of hindsight, we could perhaps argue that Tyson in his prime would have fared no better in the cage than James Toney. However, just imagine if Tyson had developed devastating takedowns and excellent submissions to compliment his striking ability. That would be some fighter!

Cuban fighter Hector Lombard resembles an in shape Tyson, with his powerfully built body and menacing prowl. For a fighter, looking the part is only a small piece of the jigsaw, but Lombard, like Tyson, possesses devastating knock out power, maybe not quite in Tyson's league, although to be fair who has? To learn that Lombard is a former Olympian may not come as a great shock, but what is surprising is that the Cuban fought not as a boxer, but as a judoka. Throughout his MMA career Lombard has been regarded as one of the most explosive and exciting fighters in the world, although in judo this was not the case.

Over time it has become clear that the best martial artists on paper do not necessarily make the best MMA fighters. It is all about how each athlete adapts their own strengths to the MMA arena and how they cope with the aspects of the sport they are less comfortable with. A lot of fighters emerge nowadays having only ever trained in MMA, but even those fighters will usually favour a particular area of the game. One judoka in particular has adapted to the cage better than all the great fighters that have come before and is the first judoka to become UFC Champion. Her name is Ronda Rousey.

CHAPTER THREE
Ronda Rousey

For a man to be told that he 'fights like a girl' would once have been a great insult. This is no longer the case since the arrival of 'Rowdy' Ronda Rousey on the MMA scene.

Ronda Rousey is the current UFC Women's Bantamweight Champion and is considered pound for pound the best female fighter on the planet.

Her mother, Ann Maria Rousey DeMars, was the first American to win a World Judo Championship with her victory in 1984. Ronda followed in her mother's footsteps by becoming a Champion of the World at junior level, although at senior level she was unable to match her mother's achievement by having to settle for a silver medal. However Ronda did set records of her own by becoming the youngest judoka to compete in the entire Olympic Games in Athens and then became the first American to win an Olympic medal in the 2008 Olympic Games in Beijing, winning a well deserved bronze.

Having been so successful in judo at a young age, Rousey was able to make the transition to MMA while still in her prime as an athlete. She made her MMA debut as an amateur on the 6th August 2010 against Hayden Munoz and within 23 seconds of the first round she had secured her first win using the armbar which was to make her famous. After

two more extremely quick wins (both by armbar) Rousey announced plans to turn professional.

On 27th March 2011, Rousey made her pro debut against the Brazilian Ediane Gomes and once again she managed to submit her opponent with the same armbar, this time in 25 seconds. Three more professional fights saw three more lightning quick armbar wins, which lead to a title shot against the Strikeforce Champion Miesha Tate. Tate had been irritated by Rousey's swift route to the top and felt that Ronda should be made to wait longer for a title shot. Rousey's reply to the bad feeling was to humiliate Tate in a one sided contest that not only ended with the inevitable armbar, but was one of the most sickening submissions ever seen inside the cage. Tate's elbow joint was literally bent to 90 degrees in the wrong direction, although to her credit she dealt with the pain tremendously well, making no real reaction except to hold her damaged arm as the announcement was made. Miesha was shown a lot of admiration and respect for her bravery that night although very little came from her opponent. With matches that involve a large amount of pre fight trash talk you will often find that once the action is over both fighters are willing to at least shake hands and on occasions become close friends. Ronda is not in the game to make friends, in fact quite the opposite. Her lack of sportsmanship is becoming almost as much of a trademark as her vicious armbar. Love her or hate her Ronda Rousey is becoming a big star and the fact that she is upsetting a lot of people only increases her status. Muhammad Ali is probably the most loved sportsman of all time, yet people often forget that he was one of the most hated in the early 1960s. Rousey is not just a good fighter, she is the complete package. She is prettier than Ali, she destroys opponents quicker than Tyson, has a colder stare than Fedor, trash talks more than Conor McGregor and her ruthless submissions make Royce Gracie appear half hearted. There's no question that Ronda has the X factor although some might say 'sex factor', illustrated by her inclusion in Maxim magazine's hot 100 list at no.29. She also once revealed that having as much sex as possible before a fight was good for a female, as it boosts testosterone levels. It's a fact that sex sells and all this extra attention has done no harm in opening some doors for Rousey. After the clash with Tate and successfully defending the title, she was signed by the world's premier organisation the UFC, making her the first female fighter to do so. Announced as the champion by UFC President Dana White, she was then matched against Liz Carmouche. Carmouche looked to have Rousey in trouble in the first round with a standing face crank but after shaking off the attack she successfully defended her title by applying the armbar to continue her first round armbar winning streak. Outside of MMA Rousey has played roles in movies such as 'Expendables 3' and 'Fast and the Furious 7', starring opposite massive Hollywood stars.

Meanwhile, Cat Zingano defeated Meisha Tate and it looked very likely that Zingano would become Rousey's next opponent. It was then announced that the pair would coach against one another in 'The Ultimate Fighter 18', which would see them face off in the final match of the series. Unfortunately Zingano suffered a knee injury that required surgery and Miesha Tate stepped in as the replacement. Throughout the series Rousey and Tate came to blows on many occasions and Rousey became increasingly more frustrated with Tate's ability to come away smelling of roses, leaving her to appear as the bad guy (or girl in this case). However when it came to the fight Rousey looked a class above and despite becoming the first person to get out of the first round, Tate was given a judo master class before succumbing to yet another armbar.

After eight professional fights and eight brilliant armbar wins against world class opposition it was difficult to question her ability, although as ever there were still critics. The gripe then became 'Rousey is just a one trick pony and when she comes up against another world class grappler she will finally come unstuck'. Well her next fight against Sara McMann, the 2004 Olympic silver medallist in wrestling was bound to answer that question. The answer was a first round TKO due to a knee to the liver, a brutal finish to say the least. But the win against McMann appeared tame in comparison with the victory that followed against Alexis Davis. Within 16 seconds Davis had been on the receiving end of a flurry of punches, a knee to the mid section, a huge sweeping hip throw and 10 devastating head shots from underneath Rousey's scarf hold.

Zingano, having battled back after the knee injury and a personal tragedy was now ready for her shot against Rousey. She looked mentally and physically prepared for the challenge and even Rousey was full of respect for her opponent. However, despite Zingano's undefeated record, she only managed to last just 14 seconds against the ruthless Rousey. Zingano's flying knee strike and attemped takedown in the opening seconds of the fight worked in Rousey's favour as her judo background naturally enabled her to immediately turn the tables and end up in the top position. Without hesitation Rousey pounced on Zingano's outstretched arm like a predator going in for the kill which left Zingano frantically tapping. Another armbar, although this one was a slight variation on her usual technique, but still an armbar nonetheless.

So far Rousey has answered all the questions asked of her and it is difficult to deny that she is fast becoming an MMA legend. With her spectacular throws and of course her devastating armbar, she has done more for the popularity of judo than any judoka before her.

Her most recent win against Bethe Correia at UFC 190 on 1st August 2015, came by way of knockout. After a devastating flurry of punches and only 34 seconds into the first round, Correia ended up face down unconscious on the canvas. Correia was supposed to have an advantage in the striking department but, once again, Rousey silenced the critics. Despite the win, I think it is fair to say that Rousey is still not the best striker in the world, however in mixed martial arts the threat of her amazing grappling is enough to distract the opponent from their game plan and she always finds a way to win.

"A guy can take a punch or a kick maybe,
 but can he take being dumped on his head?"
"Judo" Gene LeBell

CHAPTER FOUR
Armbars

I cannot actually recall my first experience of armbars or armlocks as they are known in judo. All I remember is being able to apply them in practise from a very early age, although it wasn't until my teens that I would use them regularly in competition. In fact the club that I practised with was completely anti groundwork and the head coach had one simple strategy for escaping from hold downs—don't get caught in them in the first place! As a result my stand up judo became extremely good and I would always look for big throws.

In the early days I would rarely lose a fight and if I did, it would always be to a physically stronger or more aggressive opponent who would more often than not beat me on the ground. My opinion of groundwork back then, was that it was for those fighters with limited throwing ability, yet it wasn't until I began travelling further afield against better opposition that I realised I had been wrong. My tachi waza (standing technique) was usually good enough to compete with the best fighters in the country, but unlike me, most of these fighters were skilful on the floor as well as standing and if they managed to catch me there, I would often find myself flipped over with a well drilled technique. I vividly remember a particular contest that not only left me beaten but also in tears. The groundwork move that caught me was so painful I had no choice but to submit.

It was also a turning point in my judo career and I made it my mission to learn the move that had left me so defenceless. It wasn't long before I was using the move myself in competition and the tables began to turn. Coaches who once instructed their fighters to take me to the floor were now screaming at them to stand up. The success I was having on the floor encouraged me to develop my groundwork further and I would listen to other coaches, watch other fighters and even study videos. I enjoyed watching judo videos from a young age and one of my favourites was 'Ippon' featuring the great Neil Adams winning his World Championship in 1981. Neil was a master technician who was able to throw his opponents with any number of techniques. However, Neil's most famous move was the one with which he won his World Championship—the 'juji gatame'. Neil's juji gatame was often set up by a roll that became known as the 'Adams roll', a very similar roll to the one we all see Ronda Rousey perform now. As Neil was a British fighter, his winning armlock became extremely popular and the roll was practised in clubs on a regular basis during the eighties and nineties.

In the early nineties I became a member of the British Cadet Squad and the training sessions at the time were held at Neil Adams' judo club in Coventry, where the main man would teach us on a regular basis. Not surprisingly, many of the sessions involved drilling the juji gatame roll with the lock to finish. With such decent training partners it was easy to become very good at the technique and I went on to use it in competition on many occasions.

Over the years I found ways of using the technique from a number of positions, but although I was very good at the move, I never considered myself to be a specialist. There were other techniques both standing and on the ground that I perhaps had more success with, but it wasn't until I switched to the MMA game that things began to change.

Before Ronda Rousey burst onto the MMA scene the most successful groundwork fighters had usually come from Brazilian jiu jitsu backgrounds with the most common techniques being a 'triangle choke', a 'kimura' and probably the most common of all, the 'rear naked choke'. The rear naked choke is also a judo technique known as 'hadaka jime', but throughout my judo career I always considered it a slightly 'Mickey Mouse' move that would only work on inexperienced opponents with little defence on the ground. It always amazed me how so many MMA fighters would get caught by it, but it wasn't until later that I realised what a difference a sweaty body, the absence of a gi and a few accurate strikes would make.

Therefore the armbars and more specifically the juji gatame would get used far less often except on occasions when a transition was made from a mount position (a technique that is included in the book). Generally MMA fighters would maintain a mount position at all costs in order to finish a fight with a barrage of strikes. However a fighter well drilled in the techniques included in this book would almost invite the turn or bridge out, just like in the first Rousey vs Tate fight. When a fighter turns their back in this fashion, they instinctively protect their neck from a choke or strangle attack, but they will almost certainly leave their arms exposed for the taking. Once an arm has been caught it really makes no difference which direction the opponent moves in order to escape as they will always end up tapping from the inevitable armbar. We have seen this with most of Rousey's opponents and with Neil Adams' Japanese opponent back in 1981.

THE TECHNIQUES

OVERVIEW

The techniques demonstrated in the book are split into various sections as you can see below. We start with the basic armbar technique along with a simple throw as an example for an entry into the technique. Once in position it is very common for the opponent to keep a tight grip on the arm that is being attacked which brings us to the Breaking the Grip section that explains various methods to straighten the arm and apply the lock. We will then look at various ways into the basic position from the Mount, the Turtle and the Guard position. No matter how good your technique is there will always be somebody who is impossible to catch and it is important that you can make smooth transitions into different techniques. The triangle choke is another technique that is commonly used in MMA and is becoming more popular in judo. Later you will see in The System section how all the individual techniques work together.

CROSS ARMBAR/ JUJI GATAME

17

BREAKING THE GRIP

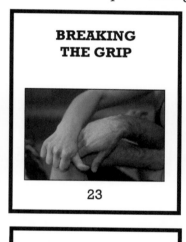

23

TRANSISTIONS FROM THE MOUNT

33

ATTACKING THE TURTLE POSITION

39

ARMBARS FROM THE GUARD POSITION

43

ARMBARS INTO TRIANGLES

51

CROSS ARMBAR/JUJI GATAME

There are a number of techniques in this book centred around the juji gatame armlock/armbar. There are others that I know that are not included in the book and I am certain there are many that I don't know, but I feel the knowledge gained from this book will help a lot of practitioners of all levels. The techniques are demonstrated by my wife, Claire, partly because she is far better looking than the guys from my gym, but she is also unofficially playing the Ronda Rousey role. Now for those who are thinking that she has only been recruited as a bit of eye candy guess again! Claire was once a member of the British Judo Squad and is also quite familiar with this particular armbar.

The Basic Position

Throw into Juji Gatame

The Basic Position

This is the basic armbar position. You can see that Claire has one leg across my throat and the other across my chest with both my arms trapped in between. To apply the armbar, Claire grips onto my nearest wrist and lays back until the arm is straight, remembering to squeeze inwards and downwards with both legs. Claire needs to make sure that my thumb is pointing upwards to ensure that the elbow joint remains against her body. If the armbar is not working, she can raise her hips in order to extend the joint even further.

Throw into Juji Gatame

REACH AROUND WAIST

From a clinch position Claire has sent her right arm deeper around my waist until it reaches my opposite side. In order to reach this far she has moved to the side so she is standing at 90 degrees to myself. At the same time she draws my right arm towards her by hooking around my tricep, which puts me in a weaker position. To stop me from simply rotating in order to face her, Claire straightens her right arm which keeps my hips facing forward and also allows her to avoid knee strikes.

STEP INTO POSITION

Claire then throws her hips across in front of mine at the same time as bending her legs in preparation for the lift.

STRAIGHTEN LEGS AND THROW

As Claire straightens her legs I begin to fly through the air. She continues to pull with her left arm and drives her right arm towards the mat.

KEEP GRIP AND STEP OVER HEAD

Claire rotates me over onto my back and immediately steps over my head in order to make the transition into the juji gatame (cross armbar). Notice that Claire has maintained the grip on my arm.

SIT BACK WITH LEG ACROSS CHEST

Claire secures the arm and sits back at the same time as throwing her right leg across my chest. Notice that Claire remains in contact with my shoulder at all times.

SINK WEIGHT ONTO SHOULDER

To stop me from rolling away she quickly sinks her weight down onto my shoulder.

Claire completes the technique and gets the submission.

BREAKING THE GRIP

We have looked at the final armbar position, but before we move on with any techniques leading up to this, it is important to warn you that in a real situation it is unlikely for the opponent to allow their arm to be straightened quite so easily and it is extremely common for them to protect it using their other arm.

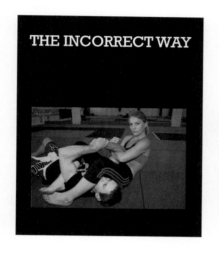

THE INCORRECT WAY

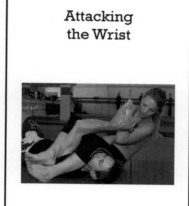

Attacking
the Wrist

Elbow Cross Over

Creating a
Wrist Attack

Using the Leg

Twisting
the Trunk

THE INCORRECT WAY

I have seen this situation thousands of times, with the fighter on top struggling to straighten the arm in order to apply the lock. Many fighters work extremely hard to get to this position but often fail to finish the job due to poor technique. The most common reason for its failure is down to the attacker's lack of knowledge on grip breaking, as they often believe that hooking inside the elbow joint and using as much brute force as possible will do the trick.

I once allowed a power lifting champion to put me in this position and he failed to break my grip. To his frustration, I easily broke his grip when the roles were reversed. Moral of the story....technique wins!

Attacking the Wrist

SLIDE UP TO WRIST LEAN TOWARDS HEAD

Attacking the wrist is usually the key to breaking the opponent's grip. If the opponent has a poor defence it can sometimes be as simple as sliding the arm up to the wrist and applying pressure like Claire is doing in the picture. Also notice how Claire is leaning towards my head to create an even weaker position for my wrist.

BREAK GRIP THEN FALL STRAIGHT BACK

As my grip breaks, Claire changes direction and falls directly backwards pulling my arm out straight.

Elbow Cross Over

Remember the story about the power lifter who failed to break my grip? Well a short time after I was training with the British judo squad and once again I allowed myself to be underneath in this very position. However this time the person latched on to my arm was not a power lifting champion but a lightweight woman. Using this very technique she straightened my arm and got the submission within seconds. For the record, it was also the technique that I used to submit the power lifter. Once again....technique wins!

Just leaning towards the head may not be enough to break the grip, so in this situation Claire tucks her right elbow behind my elbow and rotates it towards the middle of my body. If Claire continues to apply pressure to my wrist the grip will come free.

Claire breaks the grip and straightens my arm remembering to maintain a firm grip on my wrist.

Creating a Wrist Attack

ARMS LOCKED TOGETHER

On this occasion my arms are locked together making it difficult to attack the wrist of my nearest arm. There is no gap for Claire's left arm to push through (which would be even more difficult if Claire was wearing MMA gloves). So Claire maintains the pressure with her left arm as her right hand moves into position to create a gap.

SCOOP THE FINGERS

Claire makes a fist with her right hand and scoops my fingers towards her using her outstretched thumb. This bends my right wrist enough to create the gap between my arms.

(CLOSE UP VIEW)

Here we can take a closer look at what is happening when Claire draws the inside of her fist towards her. We can clearly see the gap opening up between my arms.

SWITCH LEFT HAND TO WRIST

Keeping her legs extremely tight, Claire quickly switches her left arm from the inside of my elbow joint up towards my wrist and through the gap between my arms.

LEAN TOWARDS HEAD

With my wrist in such a weak position, all Claire has to do is lean slightly towards my head and my grip is broken very easily.

GRIP BREAKS
FALL BACK STRAIGHT

Once the grip is broken, Claire changes direction and lays straight back in order to straighten my arm.

Using the Leg

PROTECTED WRIST

This time I am protecting my wrist with my other arm in order to keep it strong. So Claire changes direction and leans towards my legs instead. As a result I try to sit up in the hope of escaping.

THRUST LEFT LEG STRAIGHT

Before I manage to sit right up, Claire thrusts her left leg straight at the same time as maintaining pressure on my elbow joint. This sudden added pressure will usually break the grip.

APPLY ARMBAR FROM HERE

Because the arm comes free very quickly, Claire is able to apply the armbar without needing to adjust her position.

Twisting the Trunk

OPPONENT RESISTS LEG THRUST

Straightening the leg has failed on this occasion and I am able to maintain a strong grip on my wrist.

POST AND TWIST

So Claire reaches behind her and posts on her right arm. She then rotates her body quickly towards my legs which should free my arm ready for the submission. Claire could make this technique a lot stronger by sliding her left hand palm downwards across her right thigh. This would give her more leverage but Claire is being slightly kind to me on this technique because I am struggling with a suspected cracked rib (Unfortunately for me the grimace on my face isn't for the camera).

TURN AND FALL INTO ARMBAR

As Claire continues to rotate, my arm is straightened further. There is a chance that the armbar could be applied in this position, but it is more likely that once the grip is broken she would just lay back into the conventional armbar position.

"Punch a black belt in the face, he becomes a brown belt. Punch him again, purple..."
Carlson Gracie Snr

TRANSITIONS FROM THE MOUNT

The mount position is arguably the most dominant position in MMA, especially in professional and semi professional bouts, where strikes to the head are allowed. This is usually because the fighter on top is able to use both arms in order to unleash heavy downward shots on the opponent. It is also the position where the referee is most likely to stop the contest. However it is also a nice position from which to transition into armbars, as the fighter underneath unintentionally offers their arms to the fighter on top as they attempt to defend against strikes.

Basic Transition

Mount to Face Down Armbar

Basic Transition

GROUND AND POUND

Claire has the mount position and is looking for a stoppage with 'ground and pound'.

CONTROL THE HEAD

As I bring my hands up to protect my face Claire hooks on to my right arm with her right arm and with her left arm she pushes across my face, making it more difficult for me to bridge.

TUCK RIGHT LEG UNDER LEFT ARM

Keeping pressure inside my arm and against my head, Claire tucks her right leg tightly underneath my left arm without losing contact my body.

SWING LEFT LEG AROUND HEAD

With everything extremely tight, Claire swings her left leg around my head.

STRAIGHTEN ARM

Claire completes the transition and prepares to straighten the arm.

ARMBAR SUBMISSION

Claire applies the armbar and gets the submission.

Mount to Face Down Armbar

GROUND AND POUND

Claire once again delivers a ground and pound attack from the mount position.

OPPONENT DEFENDS

Once again I bring my arms up to protect my face.

BRIDGE AND ROLL ATTEMPT

Not wanting to take any more punishment I begin to bridge and roll. Claire seizes the opportunity to hook onto my arm and is ready to swing her left leg over my head as I roll onto my front.

ROLL WITH OPPONENT

As I roll to the left Claire follows my movement by throwing her left shin onto the back of my neck and slides her right leg underneath my body. Claire turns back towards my feet as she applies pressure to the back of my neck. As I try to remain on my front the tension against my arm increases and Claire is able to straighten my arm and gain a submission.

"It is bad in Judo to try for anything with such determination as not to be able to change your mind if necessary."
Moshe Feldenkrais, Higher Judo

ATTACKING THE TURTLE POSITION

As a former judo fighter, this is probably where I am most comfortable in groundwork. As the object in judo is to throw the opponent flat onto their back, it is extremely common for the fighter being thrown to twist out onto their front, often resulting in the turtle position. A judo fighter is usually comfortable defending from this position because there are no strikes allowed in judo and the attacking fighter will only get a short amount of time on the ground before the referee calls the fighters back onto their feet. However, as a judo fighter is faced with this position on a regular basis, they will almost certainly know a number of technique with which to submit their opponent. They are used to working against the clock, so their groundwork techniques are often explosive and well drilled.

Juji Gatame Roll

Juji Gatame Roll

RIDING THE TURTLE

I have won countless judo contests with this technique and I use it frequently in MMA. It could also be used as a continuation from the last technique (mount to face down armbar) if the opponent manages to keep a firm grip on their wrist whilst face down. An MMA fighter is unlikely to turtle up, yet it occasionally happens if they have failed with a takedown or if they have just taken a heavy body shot. In this case, the attacking fighter needs to gain control of their opponent's back quickly. Often this is done by tucking both legs inside the opponent's thighs, but for the juji gatame roll it is better to only hook one leg inside.

Here, Claire has come around to my back and quickly hooked her right leg inside my right thigh at the same time as keeping downward pressure on my back. This makes it far more difficult for me to stand up and get away.

FALL ONTO SHOULDER/PRESSURE ON NECK

Claire uses her momentum into the technique to fall onto her left shoulder and turns to look in the direction of my feet. She continues to apply as much pressure as possible onto the back of my neck with her shin so that I am unable to posture up. Claire also continues to apply pressure onto the inside of my elbow joint and if my arm comes free at this point she could apply the lock face down.

ROLL THE OPPONENT

In one movement Claire hooks my right arm with her left as she falls to the side and swings her left shin across the back of my neck. Notice how she posts on her right arm so that she doesn't fall directly on top of her head and how her right leg shoots underneath my body until it appears out the other side. You can just see her right foot appearing from under my body, which she can tighten by hooking her toes around my left thigh.

PUSH WITH RIGHT LEG (VIEW FROM OPPOSITE SIDE)

We continue to follow the technique from the opposite side of the body as we can see more clearly how Claire finishes the move. As she continues to apply pressure to my neck and my elbow, my behind begins to rise up into the air and Claire uses her right leg to help me over. If enough pressure is applied to these areas the opponent will almost voluntarily roll to relieve the pressure.

ROLL THE OPPONENT

I am no longer able to resist the technique and I am rolled onto my back. Claire has used enough leverage to roll me over in one go but if the opponent is extremely strong and manages to remain in the turtle position then the attacker has the option of using their right arm to swing the opponent's legs in a circular motion around their head and into the same finishing position.

OPPONENT ROLLS ONTO BACK

Claire has now managed to roll me completely onto my back but she cannot remain in this position for long as it will be easy for me just to sit up and escape, especially with the momentum of the technique.

Claire quickly throws her left leg over the top of my head and applies the armbar. If I manage to hold on to my arm once the roll has been completed, Claire could use one of the grip breaks that appear earlier on in the book.

ARMBARS FROM GUARD POSITION

To an untrained spectator, the guard position (the bottom position with the opponent between the legs) looks very much like a losing position. However, any decent ground fighter would know that the guard position could be used to their advantage and there are many ways with which to score from here. In Brazilian Jiu Jitsu many fighters would choose to fight from this position, whereas in judo or MMA a fighter would generally only end up here as a result of being thrown or taken down. Either way it is very important to have a number of techniques from the bottom and we will look at three techniques transitioning into the same armbar.

Juji Gatame
from Guard

Stacked
from Guard

Guard into
Juji Gatame Roll

Juji Gatame from Guard

CONTROL THE WRIST

In Brazilian Jiu Jitsu this could be seen as a 50/50 situation with me looking to pass Claire's guard and Claire looking to destroy my base (low/wide balance) in order to gain an advantage. In MMA I would be more dangerous with strikes from this position, so Claire needs to gain wrist control as soon as possible. Here Claire has gained control of my right arm and has pinned it tight to her body.

HIPS TO LEFT & TURN

Claire uses her left foot on the floor so that she can move her hips slightly over to the left. This exposes a small gap between my legs which she fills with her right hand as she quickly reaches behind my left knee. Claire then uses the hook behind my knee to pull herself 90 degrees to the right. At the same time, she drives her right leg up underneath my armpit making sure that my right arm remains pinned against her body at all times.

CONTROL ARM AND LEFT LEG ACROSS FACE

Claire successfully destroys my base with her turning action and with the strong drive with her right leg underneath my left arm pit. Notice the direction that Claire turns her right foot in order to topple me forwards. The tight control on my right arm prevents me from stopping the technique as I am forced into a forward roll. Finally her left leg comes across the front of my face as she begins to transition for the armbar.

TIGHTEN YOUR LEGS

As soon as I land on my back, Claire tightens her legs and prepares to straighten my arm.

EXTEND THE ARM

Claire extends my arm remembering to keep my thumb pointing upwards and her legs nice and tight.

Stacked from Guard Position

SHIFT HIPS AND REACH INSIDE KNEE

Once again I find myself inside Claire's guard and like before she gains wrist control and secures my right arm tight to her body. She then begins to shift her hips to the left and reaches inside my left knee.

OPPONENT'S BASE STILL STRONG

Claire's right leg has made contact with my left arm pit and the grip on my right arm remains tight, but this time the technique is lacking the explosive power that was there last time. As a result she makes less rotation and my base is still strong.

GETTING STACKED

Despite my strong base, Claire continues with the technique. This time when she brings her left leg across my face I am not off balance as I was the last time, so instead of falling onto my back, I am instead able to improve my base (notice my wide legs for better stability) and apply pressure downwards on top of Claire. This is known as 'getting stacked' and is extremely weak for the fighter underneath.

SLIP OUT THE BACK DOOR

Before I have the chance to escape, Claire regains the advantage by hooking her right hand underneath my knee and rotates herself to the right and under my body (she can still hook inside the knee even if I remain in a kneeling position). Once she pulls herself half way through she can switch her right hand to the outside of my right thigh in order to complete the rotation, a technique sometimes referred to as 'slipping out the back door'. Throughout the move, Claire must keep a firm grip on my arm and remain tight with the legs.

SLIP OUT THE BACK DOOR (VIEW FROM OPPOSITE SIDE)

We are now looking at the technique from the opposite side of the body and the position is now very similar to the one we looked at during the juji gatame roll from the turtle position.

Claire gives a final push onto my right thigh as she emerges out from underneath my body.

SWING LEGS AROUND HEAD 1

We have switched back across to the other side now so that we can look at the position of Claire's legs. If you remember, when Claire was attempting the juji gatame roll from the turtle position her left shin was applying pressure to the back of my neck, but this time her leg is still across my face from the original attempt. This means that the juji gatame roll may be slightly more difficult, so Claire will choose to swing my legs around her head (this version was mentioned earlier but not demonstrated).

SWING LEGS AROUND HEAD 2

Claire takes hold of my nearest leg and starts to draw my legs around her head. If my knees are slightly closer together, she may choose to reach for my left leg which can allow her slightly more control.

ARM BAR SUBMISSION

As soon as I end up on my back, Claire wastes no time in extending my arm and gaining the submission.

Guard into Juji Gatame

OPPONENT THROWING PUNCHES

I am inside Claire's guard, but this time it is slightly more difficult for her to take control, as I am posturing up in order to throw some shots towards her head.

DEFLECT PUNCH TO SIDE

Claire is ready for the punch and instead of trying to block the shot she times it so that she is able to deflect it. You do not need to be physically strong in order to do this.

CONTROL ARM AND SLIP HIPS TO LEFT

The momentum from my punch has sent me off balance. Claire on the other hand has kept control of my arm while slipping her hips to the left and slightly turning to face me.

THROW LEFT LEG ACROSS BACK

Before I have a chance to recover, Claire throws her left leg across my back. Here she uses the inside of her leg but another option is to place the bottom of the foot on the back or the hip. This action is used as a step to climb onto the opponent's back.

CLIMB ONTO THE BACK

Using her leg (or foot), Claire flicks herself up onto my back. I will try to posture back up at the first opportunity, so this cannot be a slow movement otherwise Claire will find herself back to square one with me inside her guard.

POSITION FOR THE ROLL

The climb to the back must be quick until Claire reaches this position. If necessary she can now slow everything down as it is almost impossible for me to posture back up once Claire's left shin is on the back of my neck and she is facing my feet.

ROLL THE OPPONENT

With the pressure against my arm and the back of my neck, it is easy for Claire to continue the roll. Remember, if the opponent doesn't go over immediately, the option is always there to swing the legs around the head.

BRING LEFT LEG ACROSS FACE

As soon as I roll onto my back, Claire brings her left leg quickly across my face without releasing the pressure from my arm.

Claire pulls my arm straight into the perfect armbar position.

ARMBARS INTO TRIANGLES

This book is obviously centred around armbars, but even the best fighters will find that on occasions their favourite technique just isn't working. This could simply be due to the size or shape of a certain opponent and sometimes when a fighter has such a reputation for winning with a particular technique, every opponent will study ways to defend against it. That is why it is important to have a Plan B in case this situation arises. My favourite judo throw was the tomoe nage (stomach throw/circle throw), which I used very often in competition and have thrown world class fighters with. If I trained at a foreign training camp where I wasn't so well known I would throw almost everyone that I practised with using the technique. After a while I could feel opponents trying to anticipate when I would attack and had slightly more success at defending against it. When this happened I found it was then a lot easier to score with other throws as their mind was occupied with defending against the tomoe nage. So we will now look at a couple transitions from the armbar into triangle chokes. The triangle choke is one of the most common submissions seen in mixed martial arts.

Transition to Triangle Choke

Transition to Reverse Triangle Choke

Transition to Triangle Choke

UNABLE TO BREAK GRIP

Claire works to straighten my arm but I am doing a good job of protecting it.

BOTH LEGS ABOVE LEFT ARM

As Claire works to free my arm, both legs have somehow ended up above my left arm. This may happen accidentally when I attempt to escape, or it could be that Claire pushes her right leg though the gap towards my head as she prepares to make the transition.

REMOVE LEG AND POST TO SIDE

Claire removes her left leg from across my neck and posts it out to the side. This is in case I attempt to escape by using a bridge. Her right leg continues to keep control across my body.

SLIDE LEFT HAND BEHIND HEAD AND CATCH SHIN

Claire keeps a secure grip on my arm using her right arm and slides her left hand underneath my neck. She then catches hold of her right shin and pulls it tight against the side of my neck.

FALL BACK AND COMPLETE TRIANGLE

Claire continues to squeeze her leg against the side of my neck as she fall backwards. With very few options I attempt to posture up and escape, but this only results in the technique becoming even tighter. Eventually Claire straightens her left leg before curling the back of her knee across her right ankle leaving me with just two options... tap out or pass out!

Transition to Reverse Triangle Choke

UNABLE TO BREAK GRIP

Claire finds it difficult to straighten my arm once again.

BOTH LEGS BELOW LEFT ARM

This time Claire's legs are both below my left arm. Again this can happen accidentally as I attempt to escape or Claire may choose to push her left leg through the gap and under my arm as she prepares for the transition.

REMOVE LEG & TUCK UNDER RIBS

Claire removes her right leg from across my body and she tucks her foot just underneath my ribs. As she moves her position she slightly releases the pressure with her left leg.

RELEASE PRESSURE TO SET A TRAP

Claire keeps a firm grip on my arm and falls onto her side. The lack of pressure across the front of my neck entices me to sit up in the hope of escaping. However, Claire is leading me into a trap and as I lift my shoulders she starts to make her transition by sliding her right leg underneath my body.

CAPTURE ARM AND HOOK YOUR LEG

From the opposite angle it is easier to see what happens when Claire's leg appears from underneath my body. As Claire drives her leg through she catches my left arm and pulls it tight towards her. Finally she places her left foot behind her right knee before curling her bottom leg back to apply the strangle.

THE SYSTEM

DOMINIC KING'S
ARMBAR SYSTEM
PUTTING IT ALL TOGETHER

ARMBAR

THROW • BREAK THE GRIP • MOUNT • TURTLE • SWITCH THE ATTACK • GUARD

"When I was sixteen I had an epiphany about my matwork. Until then, I had just been memorising different moves. I would think, OK, the person's here I'll try this. The person moves this way I'll try that. All the moves were separate in my head.

Then one day, I went for an armbar, and my opponent shifted, making it impossible for me to execute that move. I got stacked, then I realized that in defending against my attack, my opponent had perfectly positioned me to carry out a different type of armbar. It was like I just landed in the middle of that move. I called it the Juji Squish Roll.

That was the first time I linked two different techniques on the ground, and then I realised you could do that with everything. From that moment on, I was constantly looking for ways that I could connect seemingly unconnected moves. Instead of being frustrated by what most people saw as a failure, I looked at it as an opportunity to create something new."

Ronda Rousey, My Fight Your Fight

START YOUR ATTACK

THROW

TURTLE

MOUNT

GUARD
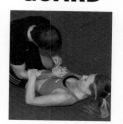

OPPONENT DEFENDS

BREAK THE GRIP

UNBREAKABLE GRIP

SWITCH THE ATTACK

SUBMISSION

JUJI GATAME/ARMBAR

TRIANGLE CHOKE

THROW • MOUNT
BREAK THE GRIP
ARM BAR
SWITCH THE ATTACK
GUARD • TURTLE

ARMBAR FLOWCHARTS

The five Armbar Flowcharts show how the techniques you've learned come together in pursuit of the armbar submission. So, rather than just a series of techniques you'll have a systematic approach to achieving a submission with juji gatame/armbar or be able to seize the opportunity for applying a triangle choke while your oppnent is distracted by trying to defend your armbar attack.

Once you're familiar with the techniques, the Armbar Flowcharts provide a quick summary and revision of the flow and also show how the techniques interrelate by highlighting the choice points where you can flow from one to another.

A useful exercise while you are looking through the flowcharts is to explore all the possible variations and mentally rehearse different scenarios.

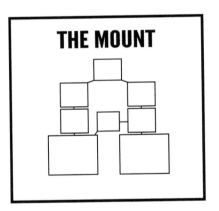

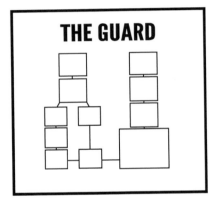

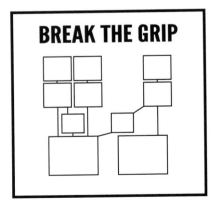

ARMBAR SYSTEM

THROW   TURTLE

PAGE 20

STANDING CLINCH

From the clinch you can throw your opponent and simply flow straight into the armbar.

They may turtle up but the juji gatame roll is very effective. If they resist the roll you can swing their legs over your head and continue into the armbar.

PAGE 39

RIDING THE TURTLE

Throws to Floor

ARMBAR SYSTEM

Hook in and Control

Controls and Sit Back

PAGE 47

Swing Legs Over

Juji Gatame Roll

JUJI GATAME

THE MOUNT

PAGE 33
GROUND AND POUND

As your opponent defends they will offer up an arm or try to turn away. Take the arm or roll with them when they turn and be ready to switch to the juji gatame roll if they keep rolling.

PAGE 34
Control the Head

PAGE 36
Bridge & Roll Attempt

Sit and Turn

PAGE 40
Juji Gatame Roll

Roll with Opponent

JUJI GATAME

ARMBAR SYSTEM

THROW THE GRIP MOUNT
BREAK THE GRIP
ARM BAR
GUARD SWITCH THE ATTACK TURTLE

Copyright © 2015
by Dominic King

FACE DOWN ARMBAR

THE GUARD

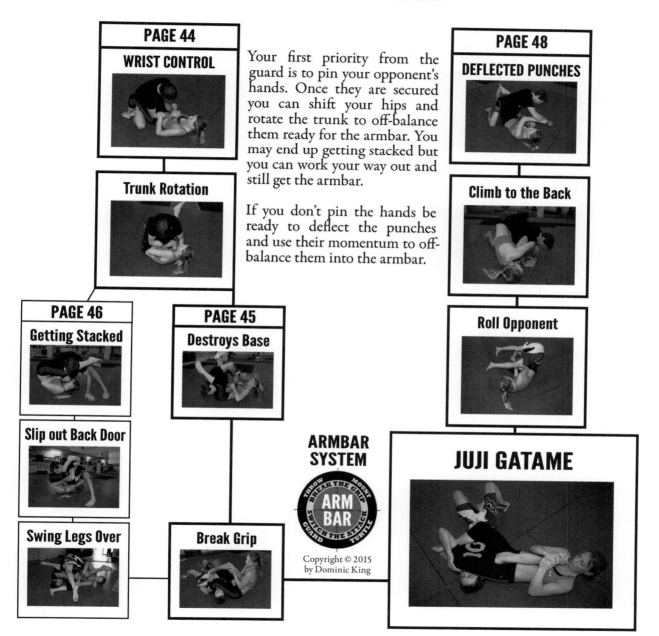

PAGE 44

WRIST CONTROL

Trunk Rotation

PAGE 46

Getting Stacked

Slip out Back Door

Swing Legs Over

PAGE 45

Destroys Base

Break Grip

Your first priority from the guard is to pin your opponent's hands. Once they are secured you can shift your hips and rotate the trunk to off-balance them ready for the armbar. You may end up getting stacked but you can work your way out and still get the armbar.

If you don't pin the hands be ready to deflect the punches and use their momentum to off-balance them into the armbar.

ARMBAR SYSTEM

THROW · BREAK THE GRIP · MOUNT
ARM BAR
GUARD · SWITCH THE ATTACK · TURTLE

Copyright © 2015
by Dominic King

PAGE 48

DEFLECTED PUNCHES

Climb to the Back

Roll Opponent

JUJI GATAME

65

BREAK THE GRIP

PAGE 25
BASIC GRIP

PAGE 28
ARMS TOGETHER

Your opponent will usually defend by gripping his hands or arms together. The basic grip can be broken by attacking the wrist but if you need more leverage use the elbow cross over. If his arms are close together you'll need to create a wrist attack and make a gap. If they are protecting their wrist use your leg to add strength and twist your trunk if you need more leverage.

If you're unable to break the grip then you can switch the attack and go for a triangle choke - see next page.

PAGE 30
PROTECTED WRIST

Attacking the Wrist

Create a Wrist Attack

Using the Leg

PAGE 26
Elbow Cross Over

PAGE 31
Twist the Trunk

JUJI GATAME

ARMBAR SYSTEM

THROW • MOUNT • BREAK THE GRIP • SWITCH THE ATTACK • GUARD • TURTLE

ARM BAR

Copyright © 2015 by Dominic King

ARMBAR WITH LEG

SWITCH THE ATTACK

PAGE 51

UNBREAKABLE GRIP

PAGE 52

Legs Above Arm

If you're able to break the grip or while your opponent is busy defending your armbar attack you can switch your attack by threading one of your legs between his arms and finishing with a triangle choke.

PAGE 54

Legs Below Arm

Post & Capture Head

Set a Trap

TRIANGLE CHOKE

ARMBAR SYSTEM

THROW · MOUNT · BREAK THE GRIP · ARM BAR · SWITCH THE ATTACK · GUARD · TURTLE

REVERSE TRIANGLE

NOTES

NOTES

NOTES

NOTES

NOTES

NOTES

NOTES

Printed in Poland
by Amazon Fulfillment
Poland Sp. z o.o., Wrocław